How do I feel about

MY PARENTS' DIVORCE

Julia Cole

COPPER BEECH BOOKS • BROOKFIELD, CONNECTICUT

Designed and produced by
Aladdin Books Ltd
28 Percy Street
London W1P 0LD

First published in the United States
in 1998 by
Copper Beech Books,
an imprint of
The Millbrook Press
2 Old New Milford Road
Brookfield, Connecticut 06804

Printed in Belgium
5 4 3 2 1

Designer   Tessa Barwick
Editor   Sarah Levete
Illustrator   Christopher
                  O'Neill
Photographer   Roger Vlitos

**Library of Congress
Cataloging-in-Publication Data**
Cole, Julia.
My parents' divorce / Julia Cole ; illustrated by
Christopher O'Neill.
p. cm. — (How do I feel about)
Includes index.
Summary: Discusses why divorce happens, how to
cope with it, and how to deal with difficult feelings
as well as friends whose parents are divorced.
ISBN 0-7613-0869-5 (lib.bdg.)
1. Children of divorced parents—Psychology—
Juvenile literature.
2. Divorce—Juvenile literature. [1. Divorce.]
I. O'Neill, Christopher, ill. II. Title. III. Series.
HQ777.5.C635   1998 98-16956
306.89—dc21   CIP AC

Contents

Introduction

Jon, Lisa, Mark, and Sally know how it feels when a mom and dad decide to live apart. You may have a friend whose parents are separated or divorced, or your parents may have split up. Join the friends as they talk about their feelings.

I live with my dad and see my mom on weekends.

Sally is my sister. Our parents are getting a divorce.

My mom and dad are separated. I live with my mom.

Even though they're divorcing, we'll still see Dad.

JON

LISA

MARK

SALLY

What Is Divorce?

Jon is explaining that separation is when two grown-ups who have lived together decide to live apart. If they are married they may also decide to get a divorce. You may hear someone say that his or her parents have split up. This can mean that they are separated or divorced.

I don't understand the difference between divorce and separation.

Grown-ups can only divorce if they are married. They may separate first.

My parents live apart from each other. They are separated.

My parents live apart, too. They've also got a document that says they're no longer married.

Splitting up is when parents separate.

It's also when parents divorce.

▽ Splitting Up

Splitting up is when grown-ups decide to live apart. If they are married, they may decide to divorce. Grown-ups who split up usually live in separate homes. They may live alone or they may live with a new partner.

◁ Who Divorces?

Only grown-ups who have been married can get a divorce, because a divorce is a legal end to a marriage. But grown-ups who are married can still separate without getting a divorce.

Jon, tell us about your parents.

"My parents split up about four years ago. I don't see my dad anymore. I live with Mom. Because Mom and Dad never married, they didn't need to get a divorce. I don't think it matters if you call it divorce, separation, or splitting up. They all mean that two grown-ups have decided to live separately."

5

What Happens?

Mark is telling Lisa that his dad is going to live somewhere else.
When Anu's parents split up, she and her dad moved.
Each situation is different, but most moms and dads want to
make sure their children will be OK. Whatever your mom and
dad do, you will still be looked after.

My dad is looking for somewhere else to live.

We've decided to live apart.

Dad and I moved to a new house.

Will I have to split up too?

One parent usually moves out.

6

You don't have to split up!

1. Matt thought divorce or separation happened right away.

2. Josie thought Matt would forget her. But he wanted to stay friends.

3. Talking helped Josie and Matt to realize that each situation is different.

Why is it different for Matt and Josie?

Matt and Josie now know that every family is different. One parent may move out before you have been told what is happening. Or your parents may tell you that they are splitting up before anything happens. Like Matt you may stay in your home, or like Josie you may have to move.

1. Sam wanted her mom and dad to stay together, but her mom was moving out.

2. Sam's parents had decided that Sam would stay with her dad.

3. Sam found it difficult to understand how her mom could leave and still love her.

Will Sam's mom still love her?

Sam's mom is going to live apart from Sam and her dad, but this doesn't mean that she will stop loving Sam. She will still see Sam regularly. Some parents stay in contact with their children a lot. Others don't visit very much, but whatever happens, they will always be your mom and dad.

▼ *What About Me?*

Sometimes your parents will decide between themselves whom you stay with or they may ask you what you think. Sometimes the courts need to help decide this. They may also decide when and if you see your other parent.

◀ *Together Again!*

The parent from whom you live apart may try to visit or to see you as much as he or she can. However, this may not always be possible. You can ask the parent with whom you live to explain the new situation.

Can he live with us in our new house?

Lisa, you live with your dad now. Do you see your mom?

"Yes. When my parents separated they decided that my sister, Meg, and I should live with Dad. We moved house and everything. But Meg and I still see Mom on weekends and during vacation."

Why Does It Happen?

Mark is telling Sally why he thinks their parents are splitting up. There can be lots of reasons why parents split up. They may not love each other in the same way as they used to, or they may meet someone else they want to be with. Whatever the reason, it doesn't mean that they will stop loving you.

▷ *Arguing Again!*

Parents can argue so much they become very unhappy. They may feel that they should part in order to stop fighting. They may decide that even though divorce or separation is upsetting, in the end it will mean that everyone can be happier.

It's quieter here than at home!

▽ *But Dad Loves Her*

Sometimes only one parent wants to live away from the other parent. If this is the case, the parent who doesn't want the other one to leave may find it difficult to accept and understand the new situation.

◁ *New Partners*

One parent may find a new friend they can talk to and get along with better. He or she may choose to live with them instead of your mom or dad. If this happens, you may feel very angry toward your parent's new partner.

1. Jo and Jim Jones were arguing over a computer game.

2. Their mom heard them arguing. She came in and yelled at them.

3. A week later, Mr. and Mrs. Jones told Jo and Jim that they were splitting up.

Are Mr. and Mrs. Jones splitting up because Jo and Jim argued?

No, definitely not. Parents who split up do so because they feel unhappy with each other. Mrs. Jones was angry with Jim and Jo, but it had nothing to do with the decision to separate from Mr. Jones. It is important to remember that you are not to blame for the separation or divorce of your parents.

▼ I Don't Understand

Sometimes the situation may be very complicated. If you can, try talking to an older brother, sister, or grandparent to help you to understand better what is happening.

Is it Mom's fault for working so hard . . .

. . .or Dad's for playing so much golf?

It's just that they aren't happy with each other anymore.

◄ Who's To Blame?

You may want to blame one of your parents if they split up. But grown-ups often decide together to separate or divorce. Even if it is just one parent's choice, blaming him or her won't help anyone.

Mark, do you understand why your parents are getting a divorce?

"Sally says it's Mom's fault for shouting at Dad. But it's not fair to blame Mom. Dad shouts at Mom, too. I think they are splitting up because they will be happier if they live apart. I'll miss Dad but it will be better if the arguments stop."

13

Difficult Feelings

Sally is at Lisa's house after school. She is asking Lisa how she felt when her parents split up. Like Sally and Lisa, you might have lots of difficult and confusing feelings if your parents separate or get a divorce.

I got upset when people said nasty things about my mom.

I still feel angry with my mom.

Why are you always saying mean things about my mom?

I hate you!

You may feel confused by other people.

You may feel very angry.

▼ Nothing's Changed

After splitting up, one or both of your parents may be sad for a while. This can be hard to understand if they have split up so they would not be upset. It can take time to stop feeling sad.

▶ In The Middle

Sometimes you may feel caught in the middle between your mom and dad. If this happens, talk to your parents about it. Why not ask them to talk to each other, instead of saying things to you about the other one?

◀ But I Want Them Both

You may feel upset and want your mom and dad to stay together, even if they have been sad. You may feel angry with the parent with whom you live and want to blame him or her for the situation. These feelings are quite natural.

1. Billy was angry that his parents were splitting up. He didn't want them to.

2. At school, Billy wouldn't do what his teacher asked him to do.

3. Billy told his teacher that he felt as if nobody cared about his feelings.

Why did Billy misbehave at school?

Billy was feeling unhappy and angry. He wanted somebody to take notice of his feelings. But Billy didn't have to misbehave in order to get attention. He could have told his parents or his teacher how he felt. It is better to talk about your feelings, rather than get angry or even get into trouble.

16

▼ Why Isn't It OK Now?

Sometimes your mom and dad may argue, even if they don't live together anymore. It can take time for them to sort out how to share the things they used to own together. They may also still feel angry with each other.

◄ Other People

Sometimes other people don't understand the situation and may say upsetting things about your parents. However hard it is, try to ignore such comments. Instead, talk to good friends and other members of your family.

Why do they still argue?

Sally, how do you cope with your difficult feelings?

"I still feel a bit angry with my mom but I feel better about it now. It was good talking to Lisa, even though I know it won't make Mom and Dad get back together again."

Feeling OK

Getting used to changes in the family is not easy. At first, Lisa missed her mom, but she prefers it now because both her parents are happier. Jon took a while to get used to all the changes. He misses seeing his dad, but feels better about things now.

It's better now because everybody is happier.

Can I be happy if Dad is sad?

It took a long time to get used to the changes after Dad left.

It's OK to enjoy yourself.

18

Friends can make you feel better.

▽ In Touch

If you miss your mom or dad, why not write him or her a letter or draw a picture? It may not always be possible to see him or her, but there is nothing wrong in wanting to keep in touch with your other parent.

◁ No Change

Sometimes you have to accept a situation, even though it may not be what you want. If you talk to your parent about your feelings, he or she will be able to understand how you feel about the situation.

▷ Talking Helps

When parents separate or divorce, there will be lots of changes. For instance, you may spend your birthday with only one parent instead of both parents. But just because things are not the same as before doesn't mean that they can't be just as good or even better.

1. Lucy's mom and dad had split up. Lucy didn't want to see or talk to her mom.

3. Lucy's dad persuaded Lucy to talk to her mom. It made her feel better.

2. Lucy's dad tried to understand why Lucy was so angry with her mom.

Why did Lucy feel better after she had talked to her mom?

Lucy was upset that her mom had left her dad. Speaking to her mom on the telephone didn't make all of her anger and upset feelings go away, but she was glad she had spoken to her mom. A divorce or separation is upsetting for everyone, but bit by bit, sad feelings do go away as you get used to a new situation.

▼ *It's OK To Feel Sad*

If your parents split up, you may feel very confused and unhappy. Hiding your feelings can make everything seem even worse. It helps to talk to friends whose parents have also split up or to a close friend who you trust.

◄ *It's OK To Feel Happy*

If one or both of your parents are feeling sad you may think that you shouldn't enjoy yourself. It may take a while for your parents to feel OK again, but that doesn't mean that they don't want you to have fun.

Lisa, *what helped you to feel OK?*

"When Mom and Dad separated, I felt lonely so I told my best friend at school. When I felt unhappy, she and my other friend cheered me up. It helped, too, to keep doing the things I always did before, like playing on the hockey team."

Don't Forget . . .

Sally, what is your advice to someone whose parents are splitting up?

"Talk to your parents about your angry or sad feelings, and any other feelings, too! Then your mom and dad will understand better how you feel. Talk to teachers and friends, too. It's not easy, but you do begin to feel better after a while."

Mark, do you agree with Sally?

"Yes, but also don't forget how your parents feel. They don't want to make you sad. Moms and dads have to sort out what is right for them and for you, even if that means that you may all feel upset for a while. If your parents do separate or get a divorce, they are still your mom and dad. Nothing can change that."

22

Lisa, did it take you long to feel better?

"Quite a long time. Sometimes I still miss seeing my mom every day, but it's much better now because there is no more shouting. I think it helps to keep doing the things that you usually do, like playing with friends or visiting your favorite places."

Jon, how do you feel about not seeing your dad?

"It was really hard at first, but I'm not going to let it stop me from having a good time, because that wouldn't help Mom either. I like it now, with just me and Mom. And lots of friends, too!"

Index

All the photographs in this book have been posed by models. The publishers would like to thank them all.